Grammar Made Simple

Grade 2

Written by Barbara Allman
Interior Illustrations by Viki Woodworth
Cover Illustrations by Anita Dufalla

FS123301 Grammar Made Simple Grade 2
All rights reserved–Printed in the U.S.A.
Copyright © 2000 Frank Schaffer Publications
23740 Hawthorne Blvd.
Torrance, CA 90505

Table of Contents

Introduction

Grammar can foster an awareness of the importance of language in our lives. Daily grammar activities in reading, writing, listening, and speaking can help students internalize important concepts about language.

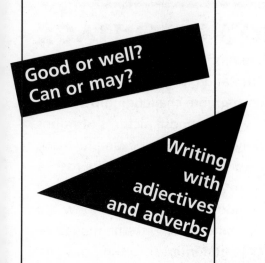

What is a sentence?

Capitalization

Good or well?
Can or may?

Writing with adjectives and adverbs

Exploring language is an important part of learning and discovery. *Grammar Made Simple Grade 2* is designed to help teachers make grammar an integral part of their language programs. Activities in this book will give second graders experience and practice in whole group, small group, and independent environments. Each section includes teacher pages with stimulating learning activities to introduce concepts to the students, as well as practice pages to cement their understanding.

Grammar Made Simple Grade 2 can be used alone or as a valuable supplement to any language program. The book focuses on parts of speech (nouns, verbs, pronouns, adjectives, articles, adverbs), sentences (subjects, predicates, kinds of sentences), capitalization, word usage, and proofreading skills. The activities are arranged sequentially, to be used in logical progression.

Acquiring language is a developmental process that links listening, speaking, reading, and writing. As you implement the ideas in this book, you will give your students opportunities to become good listeners, precise speakers, fluent readers, and expressive writers while they enjoy fun, rewarding, and meaningful activities.

Introducing Nouns

A noun is a word that names a person, place, or thing. Teach your students the definition of a noun, and give them experiences in identifying nouns. Help them differentiate between common and proper nouns, as well as singular and plural nouns.

FAIRY TALE NOUNS

Class Activity

Engage your students in a noun hunt using their favorite fairy tales and folk tales. Place several fairy tale books at a center, along with pencils and large self-sticking notes. Instruct each student to select a book and find a page that has several nouns. The student should write his or her name on a stick-on note, and list the nouns he or she found on the page, then attach the note to the page. Explain that if a page already has a list attached to it, the student should choose a different page. The following week, read some of the stories aloud and compile a class list of "fairy tale nouns" from the children's notes on chart paper.

Thumbelina Andrea	flower bird Diego	crown Drew	fairy king Terry	snow Lorena

PROPER OR COMMON?

Class Activity

Use the fairy tale nouns list compiled in the above activity to introduce common and proper nouns. Explain that a common noun names a person, place, or thing (for example, *park*). A proper noun names a special person, place, or thing and begins with a capital letter (for example, *Greenwood Park*). Have one child at a time scan the fairy tale nouns chart and draw a crayon line under a proper noun until all are underlined. Then ask for volunteers to choose a common noun from the list and give a proper noun for it, such as *King Arthur* for *king*, or *Budgy* for *bird*.

Art Project

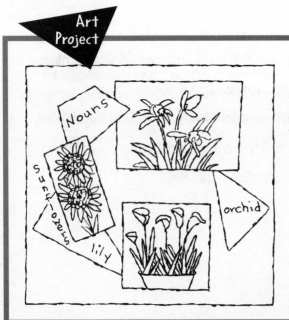

NOUN MONTAGE

Children can make montages of nouns by cutting pictures from magazines and gluing them onto sturdy paper. Make this activity more challenging by telling the children that they must choose pictures of nouns that belong to the same category. For example, a car, a boat, and a plane are all transportation; a rose, a daisy, and a tulip are all flowers. Provide scraps of colored tissue paper and wrapping paper. Show the children how to combine these with the magazine pictures to add interest to their designs.

NOUN SAFARI

Make a set of safari cards by writing nouns, verbs, and adjectives on index cards with a marking pen. Use words that identify or describe objects or activities common in the classroom (for example, *book, read, table, teacher, pencil, open, brown, hamster*). Then place the safari cards around the room near the objects they name or are associated with. Assign partners and have the children hunt with their partners for a noun. Explain that students should consult with their partners to determine if the words they find are nouns. Have the children hold up their nouns. Have each pair tell if the noun is a person, place, or thing. Replace the cards and repeat the game. Save the cards to use another time when teaching adjectives or verbs.

GROWING PLURALS

Teach your students that a singular noun names one person, place, or thing. A plural noun names more than one person, place, or thing.

singular:	flowerpot
plural:	flowerpots

Most singular nouns can be made plural by adding *s*. For example, *knights, dragons, kings, queens*. However, if a singular noun ends in *sh, ch, x, ss,* or *s* the plural is made by adding *es* (for example, *wishes, watches, foxes, kisses*).

Give your students practice in "growing" plural nouns. Write each of the following plural nouns on a length of sentence strip. Cut off the *s* or *es* ending of each word. Place the words and endings in a clean, empty flowerpot. Have the children match the words and endings to form plurals, and write each new word on a strip of green paper.

seeds	peaches	radishes	sprouts
boxes	bunches	sunglasses	gardens
rows	flowers	tools	bugs

TONGUE TWISTERS

Give children practice in identifying plural nouns. Display the tongue twisters below on sentence strips. As each tongue twister is read aloud, have a volunteer frame the plural noun with an *es* ending, using two hands. Point out that words ending in *s, ss, ch, sh,* or *x* take the ending *es*. List additional words for the children to use in composing their own tongue twisters.

Five freezing <u>foxes</u> flee.

Biscuit <u>mixes</u>. (3 times fast)

Billy brings buttered biscuits on <u>buses</u>.

Lucky Lars likes luscious <u>lunches</u>.

Pete piles park <u>passes</u>.

Book of Nouns

Nouns
I Know

by
_____
_____

Cut on the solid line and fold on the dotted lines to make a book. When you read, write the **proper nouns** and **common nouns** you find in this book.

_____

ʎq

Nouns I Know

Common Nouns
They name a person,
place, or thing.

_____

_____

_____

_____

_____

Proper Nouns
They name a special person, place, or
thing. They begin with a capital letter.

_____

_____

_____

_____

_____

FS123301 Grammar Made Simple Grade 2 ▪ © Frank Schaffer Publications, Inc.

Proper Nouns

Draw a line under the **proper nouns**.

Uncle John	Matt Hart	Ohio
Miss Sanchez	park	aunt
museum	Green Grove Library	train station
Lakeview Mall	doctor	City Science Center

Read the story. Then circle the proper nouns that need a capital letter. Write each one correctly on the lines.

On saturday, aunt marie took us to the brookside museum.

We had lunch there on the patio. Then we walked to

willow park. We took the train home from riviera station.

1. _____

2. _____

3. _____

4. _____

5. _____

Playground Nouns

A **singular noun** names one person, place, or thing. A **plural noun** names more than one person, place, or thing.
Read the nouns in the picture. Write each noun under the right heading.

One

_____

_____

_____

_____

_____

_____

More Than One

_____

_____

_____

_____

_____

_____

Name _____

More Than One

Add **s** to most nouns to make them plural.
Add **es** to nouns ending in **s, ss, x, sh,** and **ch.**
Draw lines to match the nouns and their plurals. Then write the nouns in the sentences.

treat	boxes
friend	friends
box	branches
branch	classes
class	treats

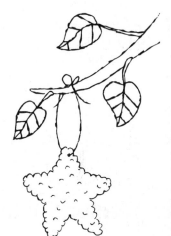

1. These _____ have bird food in them.

2. The second grade _____ are selling the boxes.

3. The _____ are for birds to eat.

4. Hang the treats in those tree _____ .

5. All of your feathered _____ will like them.

Learning About Verbs

Introduce your students to verbs with the following activities. Teach them that verbs are words that can show action or being. Help children gain experience in identifying verbs and in differentiating between past and present tense verbs.

GUESS MY VERB

Class Activity

Play a simple game with the children to introduce them to verbs. Explain that verbs are words that show action. Prepare verb cards by writing a verb on each of several index cards. See the list of suggested verbs below. Place the verb cards face down on a table and allow each child to choose one, then have the class sit in a circle with their cards. Go around the circle and have each child act out his or her verb while the rest of the class guesses the verb. When done, have the children place their cards in a pocket chart.

sit	walk	stretch	sing	hop
wiggle	read	jump	bend	swing
reach	touch	fall	skip	roll
trip	nod	write	blink	laugh

ANIMAL ACTION

Class Activity

Give your students a look at some animal action with Brian Wildsmith's picture book *Animal Games* (Oxford University Press, 1980). This book shows a variety of animals in action, describing each with a simple sentence. After reading the book, go over it again and ask the children to help you list the verbs. Then have the children look through magazines to find interesting animal pictures for a class book. Have them glue their pictures on sheets of drawing paper and write simple sentences to describe them, using the sentence pattern in Wildsmith's book. Assemble the pages and make a cover for the book with the title *Animal Action*.

Buffalo roam.

WATER MOVES

Class Activity

A creative movement exercise can help students recognize action words—verbs. Talk about the different ways the children have seen water move. For example, they may have seen a stream *flowing*, a faucet *dripping*, the surf *crashing*, a sprinkler *spraying*. List the verbs from the children's descriptions on chart paper. In a large, open space invite the children to spread out so each has his or her own space in which to move. Call out one verb from the chart at a time and invite the children to imitate water moving in that way. You might choose to play an instrumental recording as an accompaniment.

POETRY IN MOTION

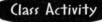
Class Activity

Give your students practice with verbs by teaching them to use this simple poetry frame. Write the following poem on the board and read it aloud. Then have the children read it with you. Draw their attention to the underlined words, pointing out that the words are verbs.

> Watch me <u>swing</u>.
>
> Watch me <u>hit</u>.
>
> Watch me <u>run</u>.
>
> Watch me <u>slide</u>.
>
> I like to <u>play</u> ball.

Next, have the class write a poem together by choosing an activity such as playing soccer, riding a bike, ice skating, or dancing. Guide the students in using the sentence pattern of the poem, substituting new verbs for the underlined words. Then challenge the children to write their own individual action poems using the pattern. Have them share their poems by reading them aloud, except for the last line. The other children can try to guess what activity the verbs describe. Have the children illustrate their poems. Display the poems and pictures on a bulletin board with the title "Poetry in Motion."

ALL KINDS OF VERBS

Class Activity

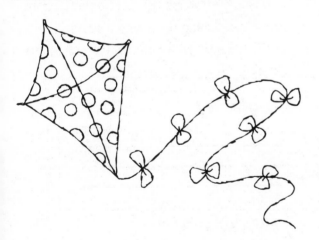

Share with your students Ruth Heller's colorful picture book about verbs, *Kites Sail High* (Putnam, 1998). Before reading the book aloud, write some of the verbs from it on index cards. Give out the cards to the children. As you read, have them listen for their verbs. When they hear them, they can hold up their cards. After finishing the story, have the children write sentences using their verbs and illustrate them. Challenge the children to make their pictures as close-up and colorful as Ruth Heller's paintings in the book.

PAST TENSE VERBS

Class Activity

Display pictures of people in action, such as athletes. Write a sentence on the board describing a picture and containing an action word in the present tense (for example, *Michelle Kwan turns in the air*). Then challenge the children to name the verb and change it to past tense by adding *d* or *ed* to the verb: *Michelle Kwan turned in the air*. Follow the same procedure for each picture. Then have the children fold a paper in half and write *Present* at the top of one half, and *Past* at the top of the other. Ask them to list the verbs from the sentences in the correct categories.

Name _____

Write the **V**erbs

Verbs are action words. Write a verb from the box to go with each picture.

grow	shines	skate
falls	chirp	bark

_____
- -
Dogs _____ .

_____
- -
Birds _____ .

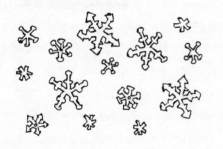

_____
- -
Snow _____ .

_____
- -
Girls _____ .

_____
- -
Sun _____ .

_____
- -
Plants _____ .

FS123301 Grammar Made Simple Grade 2 ▪ © Frank Schaffer Publications, Inc.

Water in **A**ction

A **verb** is an action word. Circle the verb in each sentence. Then write the verb in the puzzle.

Across	Down
1. Sprinklers spray the lawn.	1. We splash in the puddles.
2. The ship rolls on the ocean.	6. Two rivers run through the town.
3. Rain soaks the ground.	7. Water drips in the sink.
4. A waterfall drops over the cliff.	8. Streams flow in the mountains.
5. Waves crash on the beach.	9. The fountain shoots water.

Name _____

Teddy Bear Time

Some **verbs** tell what happened in the past.
Many verbs that tell about the past end with **ed**.

Add **ed** to the word in the box. Finish the sentence.

| stuff | A worker _____ my arms, legs, head, and body. |

| sew | Someone _____ me up. |

| brush | Another worker _____ my fur. |

| dress | Someone _____ me in a hat and bow. |

| pack | A worker _____ me in a box. |

| mail | Another worker _____ me to a little child. |

"Be" Is a Verb

The word **be** is a special verb that does not show action.
Am, is, and **are** are forms of the verb **be.**

Use **is** for one person, place, or thing.
Use **are** for more than one person, place, or thing.
Use **are** with the word **you.**
Use **am** with the word **I.**

Write **is, are,** or **am** in each sentence.

1. I _____ making a puppet.

2. Ann and Ken _____ making puppets, too.

3. We _____ having a play.

4. It _____ a play about three billy goats.

5. The play _____ on Friday.

6. You _____ invited to our play.

Name _____

Irregular Verbs

Verbs that tell about the past but do not end with **ed** are called **irregular verbs.**

<u>Now</u>	<u>In the Past</u>
eat	ate
We **eat** our lunch.	We already **ate** our breakfast.

Read each sentence. Fill in the circle beside the verb form that tells what happened in the **past.**

| 1.
Yesterday I _____ my new snow boots.

  o   wear
  o   wore | 2.
Last night three more inches of snow _____ .

  o   fell
  o   fall | 3.
While I _____ the snow piled up outside.

  o   sleep
  o   slept |
| 4.
Before school I _____ to see my friend Jan.

  o   go
  o   went | 5.
The last time it snowed, Jan _____ a snowman.

  o   built
  o   build | 6.
Yesterday, we _____ snowballs at a tree.

  o   threw
  o   throw |

 FS123301 Grammar Made Simple Grade 2 ▪ © Frank Schaffer Publications, Inc.

Discover Pronouns

The activities on this page introduce and give children practice with pronouns. Teach your students that pronouns are words that take the place of nouns. Help children gain experience in identifying the pronouns *I, you, he, she, it, they, me, him, her, us, them, our, your, my, mine,* and *their*.

MEET THE PRONOUNS
Class Activity

Use literature to introduce pronouns to your students. Explain that pronouns are words that take the place of nouns. Write the following traditional rhymes on the board and read them aloud together. Name a noun found in the rhyme and ask for a volunteer to come up and circle a word that takes the place of it. In the following rhyme, the noun *bee* is replaced by the pronoun *he*.

> There was a bee
>
> Sat on a wall.
>
> <u>He</u> said <u>he</u> could hum
>
> And that was all.

Other rhymes to use:

> Little Bo-Peep has lost <u>her</u> sheep
>
> And can't tell where to find <u>them</u>.
>
> Leave <u>them</u> alone, and <u>they</u>'ll come home
>
> Dragging <u>their</u> tails behind <u>them</u>.

> Jack Sprat could eat no fat.
>
> <u>His</u> wife could eat no lean.
>
> And so betwixt <u>them</u> both, <u>you</u> see,
>
> <u>They</u> licked the platter clean.

EXERCISE YOUR PRONOUNS
Class Activity

Write the following word-pairs exercise on the board. Ask for volunteers to come up and erase the noun from each pair, leaving the pronoun.

Jason, he	him, Grandfather	raccoon, it	Maria's, my
pie, it	Jack and Jill, they	you, girl	she, Sara
Mom, her	kittens, them	family, we	your, boy's

PRONOUNS ARE USEFUL

Help your students to understand how pronouns are useful with this read-aloud activity. Select a favorite picture book to read to the class, such as the classic *Blueberries for Sal* by Robert McCloskey (Viking, 1948). After reading the book, select a page or two to read again, this time eliminating the pronouns and replacing them with the nouns they refer to. Point out that this makes the reading longer, with many words repeated over and over. Finally, play a listening game by reading a page from the book and asking the children to give a designated signal, such as thumbs up, every time they hear a pronoun.

WHO IS THAT?

Provide magazines for the children to look through. Direct them to cut out a picture of a person's face. Have them think of a name for the person, and write an imaginary description of the person. They might answer questions about the person such as, *What does the person like to do? Where is the person going?* However, in writing their descriptions, tell them they are only allowed to write the name of the person once. The remainder of the description must use pronouns. Challenge students to use as many pronouns as possible. Have them underline and count the pronouns they use.

This is Mrs. Twinkletoes. She likes to ride her bike in the afternoon. She and her cat go everywhere together. On sunny days, they ride to the beach.

TIC-TAC-PRO

they	us	it
him	she	me
you	my	I

Play a pronoun game that will help your students remember the pronouns you have introduced. Give each student a tic-tac-toe grid reproduced from page 17. Write this list of pronouns on the board: *I, you, he, she, it, they, me, her, him, us, them, our, your, my, mine, their.* Have the children choose any nine of the pronouns and write each one in a box on their grids. When you say a word, if a student can locate it on his or her grid, the student may cover it with a slip of paper, a bean, or other marker. Students must try to cover three in a row across, down, or diagonally. Have the children clear their grids to repeat the game.

FS123301 Grammar Made Simple Grade 2 ▪ © Frank Schaffer Publications, Inc.

Tic-Tac-Pro

Play a **pronoun** game with your teacher.
Write a pronoun in each box.
Then listen for the words.
Try to cover three in a row.

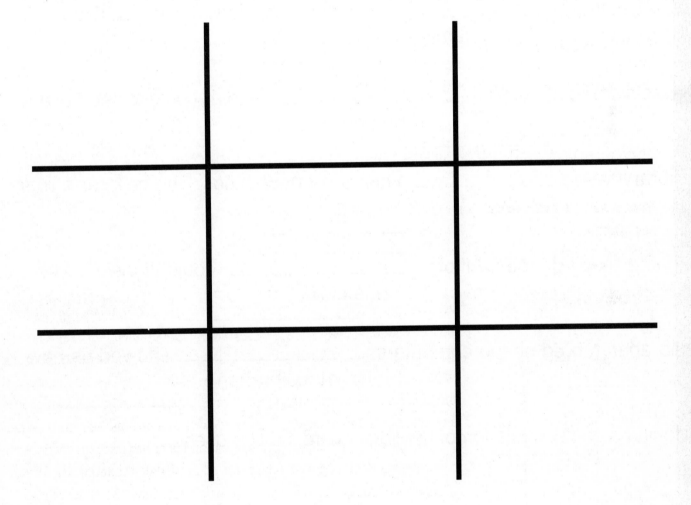

Teacher: See page 16, "Tic-Tac-Pro" for game instructions.

Pronouns

Pronouns are words that take the place of nouns. Read the sentences and the clues. Choose the best pronoun from the box to finish each sentence.

us	He	It	They	mine	we

On Saturday _____ went to the new library. Outside there
(the family)

was a crowd of people. _____ had all come to see the new
(The people)

library. _____ was full of new things. The children's room
(The library)

had a reading tepee. All of _____ could fit inside. The
(the children)

librarian turned on the computers. _____ showed us how
(the librarian)

to find a game. Maria forgot her library card, so she used _____.
(belonging to me)

FS123301 Grammar Made Simple Grade 2 ▪ © Frank Schaffer Publications, Inc.

Name _____

What Does It Stand For?

Read the sentences. Find the **pronoun** in dark letters. Write it in the box.
Draw a line to the picture that shows what word the pronoun stands for.

Pronoun   **Stands For**

Grandpa works in his garden.
He lets me help.

Grandpa showed me how to use a hoe.
It has a long handle.

"The berry plants go here," said
Grandpa.
They grow in the sun.

"Niki, get the watering can," Grandpa
told me.
"**You** can give the pots some water."

The watering can was empty.
I filled **it** with water.

Grandpa and I will eat berries.
Our hard work will taste sweet.

Introducing Adjectives

Teach your students that an adjective is a word that describes or tells something about a person, place, or thing. Give them practice in identifying adjectives, in recognizing comparative adjectives, and in using adjectives in their own writing.

NAME THAT ADJECTIVE

Class Activity

Read aloud an adjective-rich book such as *White Snow, Bright Snow* by Alvin Tresselt (Lothrop, Lee & Shepard, 1947) and invite your students to listen carefully for adjectives. On a second reading, select parts of the story and pause to ask questions that can be answered with an adjective. For example, you might ask *What kind of snowflakes? (icy, cold) What kind of sky? (clear, blue).* Write several of the adjective/noun phrases on the board. Have each child choose a phrase to write and illustrate on the front of his or her paper, and another on the back. Have them use red crayons to underline the adjectives.

BIG ADJECTIVE HUNT

Independent

Help your students tune into adjectives with a "big adjective" hunt. Give each child an index card and explain that for one whole day students are to be on the lookout for big adjectives in their reading—adjectives that contain five letters or more (or six or more, etc.). When they find big adjectives, they can write them on their cards and place the cards in a special box you have provided. At the end of the day, read aloud the big adjectives, write them on chart paper, and display the chart to encourage your students to use big adjectives in their writing.

Art Project

ADJECTIVE COLLAGES

Provide a variety of collage materials for this activity, such as colorful tissue, cotton balls, pasta shapes, craft sticks, sequins, pretzel sticks, pompoms, packing peanuts, confetti, yarn, and Easter grass. Have each child select an adjective and spell it out on sturdy paper, by gluing on collage materials that convey the adjective's meaning. For example, pretzel sticks could be used to spell *salty,* or macaroni to spell *curly.*

FS123301 Grammar Made Simple Grade 2 ▪ © Frank Schaffer Publications, Inc.

CEREAL BOX ADJECTIVES

Have your students work together in small groups on this assignment. Ask parents to help you collect empty cereal boxes. Give each group a box and instruct the children to study it, then list on a sheet of paper all the adjectives they can find written on the box. Set a timer for two or three minutes. When time is up, have the groups exchange their boxes with other groups and repeat the activity. After a few timed sessions, ask the groups to share their lists with the class.

MAKE THE MOST OF A MINUTE

Class Activity

When it is time for the class to line up, call on individual students to give adjectives describing an object you are holding in your hand. For example, if you are holding a folder, children might give adjectives such as *green*, *thin*, and *shiny*. When a child gives an adjective, he or she may get in line.

ADJECTIVE HOMEWORK

Independent

For homework, give each child a brown paper lunch bag and the following instructions.

- Place a small item from home in the bag.

- Write four adjectives about the item on the outside of the bag.

- Bring the bag with the item back to school.

Have the children try to guess what is in each bag after reading the four adjectives on the outside.

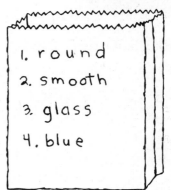

DRAWING ADJECTIVES

Class Activity

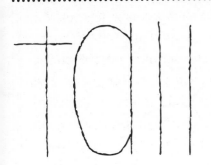

Inspire your students to write adjectives with imagination. Show students how to draw adjectives to look like their meanings. For example, the word *blue* written in blue chalk, the word *tall* written in tall letters, or the word *scary* written with a shaky hand. Have the children use sheets of drawing paper to illustrate their own adjectives.

Something About Spiders

An **adjective** is a word that describes a person, place, or thing.
Circle the adjective that describes the underlined noun in each sentence.
Write the adjectives on the lines.

1. A spider spins a sticky <u>web</u>.

2. She makes her web with silk <u>thread</u>.

3. The silk makes a strong <u>web</u>.

4. Her web is like a giant <u>net</u>.

5. She wants to trap a juicy <u>fly</u>.

6. She will catch a delicious <u>meal</u>.

_____
_____
_____
_____
_____
_____
_____
_____
_____
_____

Underline two adjectives in each sentence. Finish drawing the picture.

A big blue fly is trapped in this web.

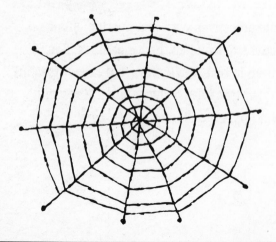

This spider has eight hairy legs.

 FS123301 Grammar Made Simple Grade 2 ■ © Frank Schaffer Publications, Inc.

Baking Bread

Some **adjectives** tell how something looks, sounds, smells, tastes, or feels. Circle the adjective in each sentence. Then write each adjective where it belongs in the chart.

1. Dad and I are baking brown bread.

2. The mix goes in a glass bowl.

3. We add the eggs and turn on the noisy mixer.

4. I pour the delicious batter into a pan.

5. Dad places it in a hot oven.

6. Good smells fill the kitchen.

7. I like the sweet smell of bread.

8. The ticking timer counts the minutes.

9. Soon, we will eat warm bread.

10. I'll put tasty jam on mine.

looks	sounds	smells	tastes	feels
1.	1.	1.	1.	1.
2.	2.	2.	2.	2.

Name _____

Words That Compare

An **adjective** that compares two things often ends in **er**.
An **adjective** that compares more than two things often ends in **est**.

Read the sentence. Use an adjective from the box to fill in the blank.

big
bigger

1. A baby blue whale is _____ than a car.

younger
youngest

2. My cat is _____ than my dog.

fast
faster

3. A jack rabbit is _____ than a horse.

slower
slowest

4. A snail is _____ than a giant turtle.

taller
tallest

5. The giraffe is the _____ of all land animals.

fast
fastest

6. The cheetah is the _____ runner of all animals.

smaller
smallest

7. A hummingbird's nest is the _____ of all.

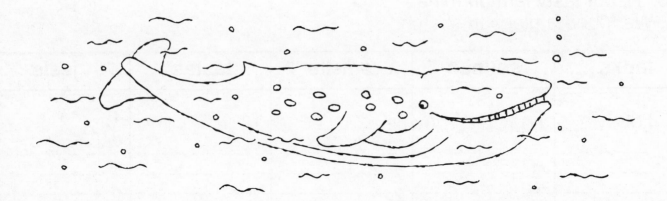

   FS123301 Grammar Made Simple Grade 2 ▪ © Frank Schaffer Publications, Inc.

Writing With Adjectives

Adjectives can make your writing more interesting.
Read each sentence. Choose an adjective from the box to describe the underlined noun. Rewrite each sentence using the adjective.

long	animal	spotted
many	quiet	Nature

1. Our class went to the <u>Center</u>.

_____

- -

_____

2. We saw nests and other <u>homes</u>.

_____

- -

_____

3. We followed a <u>path</u>.

_____

- -

_____

4. There were <u>flowers</u> blooming.

_____

- -

_____

5. We found a <u>place</u> to sketch.

_____

- -

_____

6. I drew a <u>butterfly</u> on a flower.

_____

- -

_____

Name _____

Adjectives Review

An **adjective** is a word that describes a person, place, or thing.

Fill in the circle by the adjective in each pair of words.

warm coat ○ ○   red truck ○ ○   hard brick ○ ○   pink soap ○ ○

Read each word. Fill in the circle by the best adjective to describe it.

horn
○ loud
○ happy

bear
○ furry
○ rich

pancake
○ shiny
○ round

Read each sentence. Fill in the circle by the adjective that completes the sentence.

1. Jason is _____ than Ben.

   old ○   older ○

2. Dad is the _____ in our family.

   older ○   oldest ○

3. The sun is _____ than the moon.

   bright ○   brighter ○

4. What is the _____ star of all?

   bright ○   brightest ○

FS123301 Grammar Made Simple Grade 2 ▪ © Frank Schaffer Publications, Inc.

Looking at Articles

The activities on this page introduce articles. Teach your students that *a*, *an*, and *the* before a word are called articles. These words point out a person, place, or thing. *A* is used when the following word begins with a consonant sound. *An* is used when the word following it begins with a vowel sound.

SMALL BUT IMPORTANT

Class Activity

Use literature to introduce articles to your students. Select a page from a picture book or reader that contains several articles *(a, an, the)* and make a copy of it. Make a transparency of the page from the copy. Then white out the words *a*, *an*, and *the* on the copy and make a second transparency of it. Project the first transparency and ask the children to read along with you. Then introduce the articles *a*, *an*, and *the*. Point out that these are very small but important words. Ask what would happen if all the articles were left out. Then project the second transparency and have the children read along a second time. Ask them to tell you how the writing sounded. Was it clear or confusing? Was it smooth or choppy? Do they think articles are important?

ARTICLES HUNT

Group Activity

Divide the class into groups of three children and give each group a page of newspaper. Provide highlighter pens or have the children use yellow crayons to highlight all the articles *(a, an, the)* they can find. (It isn't necessary for the students to be able to read all the words to do this.) When done, have the groups count up the number of times each article was used and compare numbers. Lead the children to conclude that articles are frequently used words.

LOLLIPOP GAME

Class Activity

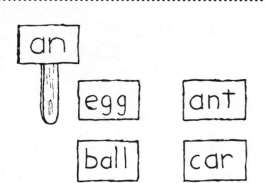

Review with students the rule for using *a* or *an*. *An* is used when the next word begins with a vowel (*a, e, i, o, u*). *A* is used when the next word begins with a consonant. Give each child a craft stick and two halves of an index card. Instruct the children to write *a* on one card and *an* on the other in large letters. Have them glue the cards to opposite sides of the stick to make a lollipop. Make several word cards of nouns that begin with vowels and of nouns that begin with consonants. As you place a word card in the pocket chart, have the children hold up their lollipop to show you which article goes with it.

A Picnic

Use **an** if the next word begins with a vowel sound: **a, e, i, o, u.**
Use **a** if the next word begins with a consonant sound.
For example: **an** aunt   **a** child

Aunt Annie is packing for a picnic. Help her finish her list of things to bring. Complete the list by writing **a** or **an** before each thing.

1. _____ egg

2. _____ basket

3. _____ blanket

4. _____ orange

5. _____ apple

6. _____ drink

7. _____ plate

8. _____ ice cube

9. _____ umbrella

10. _____ onion

11. _____ fork

12. _____ knife

13. _____ cookie

14. _____ salad

Do You Know?

A, an, and **the** are called **articles.**
Use **an** if the next word begins with a vowel sound: **a, e, i, o, u.**
Use **a** if the next word begins with a consonant sound.

Read the sentences. Write **a** or **an** in each blank.

1. Do you know _____ animal that stands for America?

2. Look on _____ American quarter to see it.

3. It is _____ bird with large wings.

4. It is _____ eagle.

5. _____ bald eagle has white feathers on its head.

6. It is _____ brave and strong bird.

Meet the Adverbs

Adverbs are words that describe verbs, adjectives, and other adverbs. Teach your students that adverbs tell how, when, or where.

FIND YOUR PARTNER

Partners

Define *adverb* for your students. Engage them in an introductory exercise. Make pairs of word cards to play this partner game. Use two colors of index cards to make the word cards. Write adverbs on one color and verbs on the other. Here are some pairs:

running fast	baked yesterday	hold carefully
going down	laughed loudly	turn right
arrive soon	read quietly	sing happily

Hide the cards around the classroom while the children are not present, then instruct them to:

1. Find a card.

2. Pair up with a person who has a different color word card.

3. Get ready to tell the class which word is a verb and which is an adverb.

The children's word pairs will likely be different than your original pairs, which will add to the fun. Have the partners read their words to the class and identify the parts of speech. Then have the children pair up with different partners and repeat the exercise.

LITERARY ADVERBS

Class Activity

Use literature to further familiarize your students with adverbs. Read aloud the following books.

▪ *Up, Up, and Away: A Book About Adverbs* by Ruth Heller (Grosset & Dunlap, 1991). The colorful, elaborate illustrations in this picture book help explain adverbs and their uses.

▪ *The Maestro Plays* by Bill Martin, Jr. (Holt, Rinehart & Winston, 1970). In this simple, patterned text, adverbs describe how the maestro plays various musical instruments. Have the children write their own version of this book. Select a different occupation (for example, *the baker bakes, the artist paints*) and ask them to contribute adverbs. Copy the story onto sentence strips. Glue the sentence strips onto a long piece of bulletin board paper. Have the children paint or draw a mural illustrating the story. Share the mural with another class.

Using Adverbs

Some **adverbs** end in **ly.** Choose an adverb from the chalkboard below for each sentence. Write the adverb in the blank.
Hint: More than one adverb will work, so choose one you like! Read your paper to a partner. Are your papers different or alike?

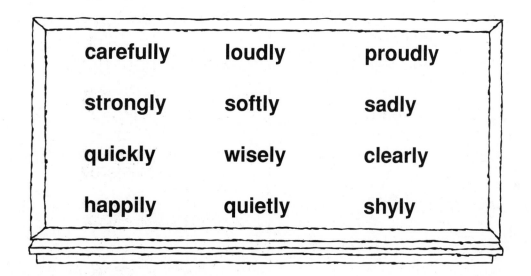

carefully	loudly	proudly
strongly	softly	sadly
quickly	wisely	clearly
happily	quietly	shyly

1. The bell rang _____.

2. The door opened _____.

3. The children walked in _____.

4. They sat down _____.

5. They all sang _____.

6. The teacher listened _____.

Find the **A**dverbs

An **adverb** is a word that describes a verb.
Adverbs tell **where, how,** or **when.**
Read the sentences. Circle the adverb in each sentence. Write the adverbs in the chart.

1. We made clay pots yesterday.

2. We dried the pots outside.

3. All the pots dried nicely.

4. We will paint our pots today.

5. We brought them inside for painting.

6. We carried the pots carefully.

7. Hold the pot gently.

8. Put the paints nearby.

9. We can paint a second coat tomorrow.

Where	How	When

FS123301 Grammar Made Simple Grade 2 ▪ © Frank Schaffer Publications, Inc.

Parts of Speech Review

Review nouns, verbs, pronouns, adjectives, articles, and adverbs with your students. Use the following activities to assess the children's mastery of parts of speech, and to provide further practice.

PROVERBS

Class Activity

Write a proverb on the board and underline key words to give your students an opportunity to review different parts of speech. Have the children write the proverb, using different colors to underline the different parts of speech. Write a color key for them to follow. For example, they may use green for nouns, blue for verbs, red for adjectives, and so on.

Here are some suggestions:

"When the <u>mouse</u> <u>laughs</u> at the <u>cat</u> there is a <u>hole</u> <u>nearby</u>." Nigerian proverb (noun, verb, noun, noun, adverb)

"To <u>make</u> a <u>beautiful</u> omelet <u>you</u> have to break <u>an</u> <u>egg</u>." Spanish proverb (verb, adjective, pronoun, article, noun)

"<u>He</u> who runs after <u>two</u> <u>rabbits</u> won't <u>catch</u> either one." Armenian proverb (pronoun, adjective, noun, verb)

"In <u>a</u> <u>good</u> <u>apple</u> you <u>sometimes</u> <u>find</u> a worm." Jewish proverb (article, adjective, noun, adverb, verb)

When the children have completed their writing papers, have them illustrate the proverb on a sheet of drawing paper.

Art Project

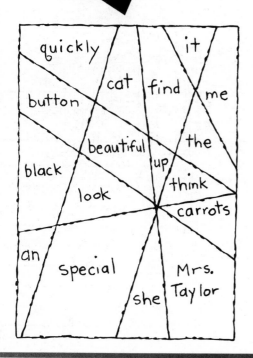

CREATIVE DESIGNS

Encourage your students to create their own unique designs in this parts of speech review activity. Instruct them to use a ruler and pencil to make seven lines on drawing paper. Demonstrate how to make the lines criss-cross and how to make the ends of each line touch the edges of the paper. If you have been collecting and categorizing words for each part of speech on charts displayed in the classroom, have the children refer to them. If not, provide a list of words that includes examples of each part of speech. Have the children write one word from the list in each space of their designs. Then explain that to finish the design, they should color all the spaces with nouns one color, those with verbs another color, and so on.

Parts of Speech Review I

Review the parts of speech and their meanings below. Read each sentence. Decide what part of speech is in **bold** print. Write the number.

1 **Noun—** a word that names a person, place, or thing.	**2** **Verb—** a word that shows action or being.	**3** **Adjective—** a word that describes a noun.

_____ Claire made a **picture**.

_____ Here is a **little** animal.

_____ This picture has a **pony**.

_____ I like the little **white** cat.

_____ We **learn** about animals.

_____ Some animals **work**.

_____ Some animals are **pets**.

_____ Ray has **three** mice.

_____ He **carried** them in a cage.

_____ What pet do you **wish** for?

FS123301 Grammar Made Simple Grade 2 ■ © Frank Schaffer Publications, Inc.

Parts of Speech Review II

Review the parts of speech and their meanings below. Read each sentence. Decide what part of speech is in **bold** print. Write the number.

1 Pronoun— a word that takes the place of a noun.	2 Adverb— a word that tells **how, when,** or **where**.	3 Article— the words **a, an** and **the**, which point out nouns.

_____ **A** winter hike is fun.

_____ **I** look for tracks in the snow.

_____ Walk **slowly** here.

_____ Look at **the** tracks.

_____ **They** are a rabbit's tracks.

_____ The rabbit went **under** a bush.

_____ It hopped **quickly.**

_____ **You** can see bird tracks here.

_____ Wait **quietly** for a minute.

_____ Did you see **an** angry bluejay?

Sentences, Subjects, and Predicates

Teach your students that a sentence is a group of words that tells a whole idea or complete thought. A sentence has a subject and a predicate. The subject tells whom or what the sentence is about. The predicate tells what the subject is doing or did.

WHAT'S THE BIG IDEA?

Center Activity

Define a *sentence* for your students as a group of words that tells a whole idea or a complete thought. Then give them practice in identifying complete sentences with this postcard activity at a center. Collect unused postcards, or cover the writing on used ones with large self-sticking white labels. On some of the postcards, write a complete sentence such as *The red cliffs are beautiful.* On other postcards, write phrases or incomplete sentences such as *The island.* Also provide two sheets of drawing paper for mats. Label one mat *sentence* and the other *not a sentence.* The mats may be laminated for durability. Instruct the children to work with partners at the center. They can take turns reading the postcards and placing them onto the mats.

HOW TO MAKE A SENTENCE

Class Activity

Share some picture books about dogs and puppies with the children to generate oral language on the topic. Then ask the children to help you create word pictures about puppies. Write the following sentence frame on the board.

_____ puppies _____

Have the children provide several descriptive words to fill in the first blank. Write the words in a list below the blank. Read each phrase that is created, pointing out that more is needed in each case to make a complete thought. Then have the children suggest things that puppies do and list them below the second blank of the sentence frame. Invite the children to create sentences by combining the different suggestions in various ways.

_____ puppies _____

frisky	look for their mother
hungry	curl up and sleep
cuddly	lick my fingers

THE SUBJECT IS . . .

Give your students practice in identifying the "naming part" of a sentence—the subject. Write the following sentences on sentence strips and cut them apart so the subject is separate from the rest of the sentence. Give a few students subject strips. One at a time, place the remaining strips in the pocket chart and have the child who has the matching subject place it in the chart to make a complete sentence. Have the student say if the subject tells who or what.

Saturday   was a rainy day.

Our picnic   was called off.

My pet finches   sing to me.

Maria and Danny   are in my class.

These old shoes   do not fit me.

We   like the library computer games.

PREDICATES ARE THE ACTION

Review with students that the predicate of a sentence is the "action part"— the part that tells what the subject is doing or did. Provide nature magazines for the children to look through. Direct the students to cut out pictures of animals in action and glue them to sheets of drawing paper. Then have each student attach a sheet of lined paper behind the picture and write a sentence about the animal. Next, have each student pass his or her paper to a person seated nearby. That person must underline the predicate of the sentence with a colored crayon. Encourage the children to discuss the sentences and predicates. Repeat the procedure until each picture has several sentences written about it. Return the pictures to their owners, and have the children share some of the sentences and their predicates with the class.

The sleepy lion watched her cubs. The mother lion sleeps by day.

THAT PREDICATE IS MIME

Write several predicate phrases on cards and distribute them to the children. Each student must try to help the class guess his or her predicate by acting it out without speaking. When the class guesses the predicate phrase, write the child's name on the board beside the predicate, to create a complete sentence. Have the class read the sentence together. Here are some suggestions:

_____ rides a bike.

_____ goes swimming.

_____ caught a fish.

_____ reads a book.

_____ makes a sandwich.

_____ wakes up.

_____ finds a coin.

_____ jumps rope.

FS123301 Grammar Made Simple Grade 2 ■ © Frank Schaffer Publications, Inc.

Is It a Sentence?

A **sentence** is a group of words that tells a complete thought.
Read the two groups of words. Write the words that make a sentence.

1. On the playground

2. Our class is on the playground.

_____

1. The yellow butterfly

2. I saw a blue butterfly.

_____

1. We are going camping.

2. At summer camp

_____

1. Dinosaurs lived long ago.

2. Big dinosaurs

_____

1. Dan is reading a new book.

2. Some new books

_____

$ubject of a $entence

The **subject** of a sentence tells whom or what the sentence is about.
Write a subject from the list in each sentence.

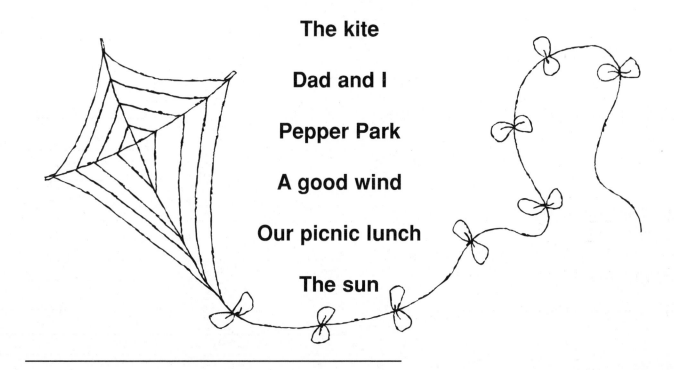

The kite

Dad and I

Pepper Park

A good wind

Our picnic lunch

The sun

1. _____ made a red kite.

2. _____ was fun to make.

3. _____ was blowing today.

4. _____ was shining brightly.

5. _____ was full of people.

6. _____ tasted great.

$\mathcal{S}$ubjects and $\mathbf{V}$erbs $\mathbf{A}$gree

Add **s** to most verbs to tell about one person, animal, or thing.
Mrs. Lopez **cooks** delicious rice and beans.
Do not add **s** to most verbs to tell about more than one noun.
The race cars **speed** around the track.

Color the leaf that has the correct verb for each sentence.

1. Grandma _____ up the leaves.   rake | rakes

2. She and I _____ them at the curb.   pile | piles

3. A gray squirrel _____ at us.   look | looks

4. The rake _____ the sidewalk.   scrape | scrapes

5. Maria and Tom _____ to jump in the leaves.   want | wants

6. Arnold _____ his bike over to watch us.   ride | rides

7. The children _____ us finish the job.   help | helps

8. Listen! The wind _____ to blow again.   begin | begins

FS123301 Grammar Made Simple Grade 2 ▪ © Frank Schaffer Publications, Inc.

Predicate

The **predicate** of a sentence tells what the subject is doing or did.
The polar bears **are swimming in icy water.**

Write a predicate from the box in each sentence.

fills up fast	**recycles newspapers**	**help collect them**
gives one class a prize	**are collected on Friday.**	

1. Our school _____ .

2. The paper bin _____ .

3. Cans and bottles _____ .

4. Parents _____ .

5. The principal _____ .

Kinds of Sentences

Familiarize your students with four kinds of sentences: statement, question, command, and exclamation. Help the children discover the distinguishing characteristics of each sentence type. With practice, children will become comfortable identifying types of sentences and writing their own sentences.

Types of Sentences

• A statement is a sentence that tells something. It begins with a capital letter and ends with a period.

• A question is a sentence that asks something. It begins with a capital letter and ends with a question mark.

• An exclamation is a sentence that shows surprise or strong feeling. It begins with a capital letter and ends with an exclamation point.

• A command is a sentence that tells someone to do something. It begins with a capital letter and ends with a period.

MAKE YOUR MARK

 Creative Movement

Provide your students with a kinesthetic experience to help them focus on the punctuation differences among the four types of sentences. Explain to the students that they are going to move like punctuation marks. Read various types of sentences while the children listen carefully. After each sentence is read, ask students to show the movement that represents the proper punctuation mark. Emphasize that in order to do this, students must think about the *kind* of sentence they hear. If they hear a question, they will know the sentence uses a question mark. If they hear surprise, they will need an exclamation point, and so on. Use the following movements or modify them to suit your situation.

Exclamation point: standing straight, jump straight up once

Period: stamp your foot

Question mark: bend torso to one side, stamp your foot

SENTENCE CENTER

This activity will give your students practice in identifying different types of sentences. Place several library books at a grammar center, along with pencils and a pad of small self-sticking notes. Post a reminder with definitions for each type of sentence: statement, question, exclamation, and command. Instruct the children to choose books to read and as they do so, look for four different kinds of sentences. They can write *statement, question, exclamation,* or *command,* initial the self-sticking notes, and place them on the pages where they found the sentences. If you wish, establish a point system as a challenge. Tell the children they can earn up to five points—one point for a statement, question, or exclamation, and two points for a command.

MUSICAL MARKS

Use a classroom set of rhythm instruments for this fun activity. Divide the class into groups of three. Have each member choose a different rhythm instrument. Assign each group an easy reader from the library such as *Grasshopper on the Road* by Arnold Lobel (Harper & Row, 1978). Be sure the text contains different types of sentences that use exclamation points, question marks, and periods. Have the groups practice doing a reading from their books, using their instruments as sound effects to indicate the punctuation at the end of each sentence. When groups are prepared, each may present its reading, complete with "soundtrack," to the class.

I'M WORDLESS

Interesting and exciting wordless picture books can give students practice in writing different types of sentences. Have the children work in small groups of three for this activity. Assign each group a wordless picture book (see literature suggestions below). Have the groups "read" their stories together by telling them aloud. Then challenge the children to write short text for each page of their stories. This can be done on large-size self-sticking notes placed on the page. The challenge is to use a variety of sentence types when they write: statements, questions, exclamations, and commands. Share one of the stories with the class each day.

Literature Suggestions

Carl Goes Shopping by Alexandra Day (Farrar, Straus, Giroux, 1989).

Early Morning in the Barn by Nancy Tafuri (Greenwillow, 1983).

Good Dog, Carl by Alexandra Day (Green Tiger, 1985).

Here Comes Alex Pumpernickel! by Fernando Krahn (Little, Brown, 1981).

Sleep Tight, Alex Pumpernickel by Fernando Krahn. (Little, Brown, 1982).

The Snowman by Raymond Briggs (Random House, 1978).

Name _____

♪tatements

A **statement** is a sentence that tells something. A statement begins with a capital letter and ends with a period. Example:

Rain and sunlight make a rainbow**.**

Write each statement correctly.

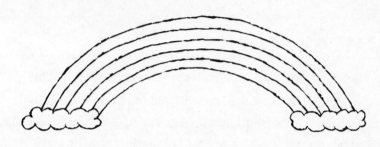

1. we see a rainbow

_____

- -

_____

2. there must be rain and sun

_____

- -

_____

3. sunlight has many colors

_____

- -

_____

4. raindrops split the sunlight

_____

- -

_____

5. we see the colors

_____

- -

_____

6. they make a rainbow

_____

- -

_____

FS123301 Grammar Made Simple Grade 2 ▪ © Frank Schaffer Publications, Inc.

Questions

A **question** is a sentence that asks something. A question begins with a capital letter and ends with a question mark. Example:
What is your favorite bird**?**

Read the story to find out about penguins.

Penguins

Penguins are seabirds, but they cannot fly. They are very good swimmers and divers. They use their wings like flippers. Penguins live in the icy seas. A thick coat of fat keeps them warm. Penguin eggs and chicks need lots of care. Penguin parents take turns caring for them.

Write three questions about what you read. Give them to a partner to write the answers on the lines below each question.

1. _____

_____

_____

2. _____

_____

_____

3. _____

_____

_____

Exclamations

An **exclamation** is a sentence that shows surprise or strong feeling. An exclamation begins with a capital letter. It ends with an **exclamation point.** Example:

We won the game**!**

Write an exclamation from the box for each picture.
Use a capital letter and an exclamation point.

what a mess	**watch out**	**wake up**
look who's here	**let's go**	**watch me**

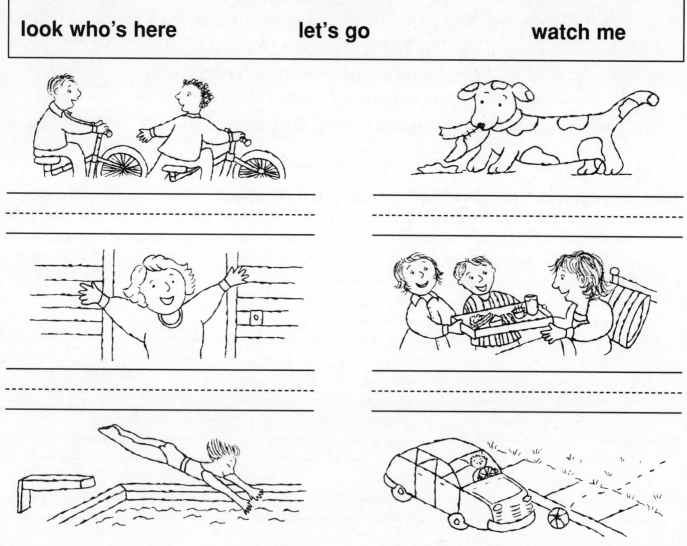

Commands

A **command** is a sentence that gives an order. A command begins with a capital letter. It ends with a **period.** Example:

Wear your hat**.**

Write a command from the box for each picture.
Use a capital letter and a period.

close the window	**hang it here**	**open your books**
wash your hands	**have one**	**ring the bell**

Word Order

The order of words in a sentence can change the meaning. Example:

Is Carla going with us?
Carla is going with us.

Write a statement and a question for each set of words.

read   her   Belle   can   book

1. ---

_____

2. ---

train   this   go   does   depot   to   the

1. ---

_____

2. ---

playing   are   Mark   Lisa   and   baseball

1. ---

_____

2. ---

FS123301 Grammar Made Simple Grade 2 ■ © Frank Schaffer Publications, Inc.

Quotation Marks

Quotation marks go around the words that someone speaks in a sentence. Example:

Brad said, "This pencil is yours."

"Thank you," said Amy.

Read the story. Put quotation marks around the words that someone speaks.

Three Billy Goats Gruff

Who is crossing my bridge? asked the Troll.

It is little Billy Goat Gruff, answered the goat.

I will eat you up, said the Troll.

The little goat said, Wait for the second Billy Goat Gruff. He's much bigger than I.

So the Troll waited for the next Billy Goat Gruff.

Now who is crossing my bridge? asked the Troll.

I am the second Billy Goat Gruff, answered the goat.

I will eat you up, said the Troll.

The second goat said, Wait for the third Billy Goat Gruff. He's much bigger.

Thinking he would get a bigger meal, the Troll waited.

Who is tramping across my bridge? asked the Troll.

I am the third Billy Goat Gruff, answered the next goat.

The Troll growled, I am coming to eat you up!

Oh no, you're not, said the biggest Billy Goat Gruff. And he tossed the Troll off the bridge with his big horns.

Capitalization

Make your students aware of some of the times when a capital letter is required: at the beginning of a sentence, for the word *I*, for initials, in titles, in days of the week and their abbreviations, in names of holidays, and in proper names of people, places, and things.

PROPER NAMES
Class Activity

Begin a classroom collection of business cards from a variety of sources. Ask parents to contribute their business cards as well. Give the children an opportunity to study the cards and ask them to tell you what information is on the cards. Elicit that business cards have names of people and businesses on them. Ask the children to tell you which words are capitalized on their cards. Lead the children to conclude that proper names of people, places, and things begin with a capital letter.

Have the children practice capitalizing proper names as they design their own "business cards," giving their names, occupations (student), classroom number, and school.

USING A MAP
Class Activity

At a writing center, post a map of your city, town, or local area for students to study and use in this activity. Discuss various places that are shown and labeled on the map. Point out to the children that names of parks, schools, roads, freeways, and so on are proper names and take a capital letter at the beginning. Have students practice capitalization by composing on their own five sentences using the names on the map.

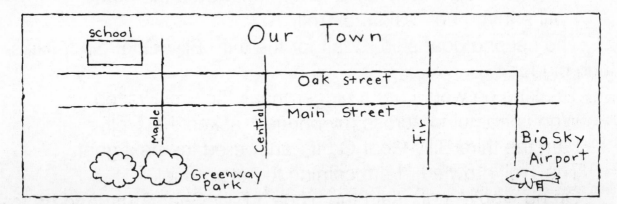

HOLIDAYS
Center Activity

Ask parents to contribute old wall calendars for use in your writing center. Children may use them to make lists of capitalized words: the months of the year and the names of holidays. Have students copy the words from the calendars for practice.

LOOK IN A BOOK

Make a class chart to categorize words that children find with capital letters. Set a timer for five minutes and instruct the children to look through books of their choice. Have each student list at least five words that have a capital letter. On chart paper, make headings such as *beginning of sentence, proper name of a person, proper name of a place, proper name of a thing, day, month, word in a title,* and so on. When the time is up, have the children tell you their words and where they belong on the chart.

BIRTHDAY LIST

Give children practice in capitalizing the months of the year by asking them to fold a sheet of paper in half three times. This will make 16 boxes, front and back. Have them write a month of the year in each box and cross out the remaining four boxes. Then allow the children to circulate around the room to find a person to sign each box. A child can only sign the box that is his or her birthday month. After several minutes, take a poll to find out if it was possible to fill all the boxes. If not, which ones were blank?

January Suzi	February Bobby
March Mary	April Alan
May Ben	June
July	August

TITLE GRAPH

In this literature activity, children can practice writing titles using capital letters. Select an author of the week for this activity and provide various titles written by him or her. Have the children read the books independently, and read others aloud to the class during the week. Then give each child an index card to write the title of his or her favorite book. Point out that capital letters are used in the important words in a title. Attach the cards to a piece of bulletin board paper, in rows according to title. This will make a bar graph showing the favorite titles chosen by the class.

Capitals in Sentences

Unscramble the words to make **sentences**. Write the words in order.
Begin each sentence with a capital letter.

1. sun   was   out   this   morning   the

   _____

   -

   _____

2. see   now   we   gray   clouds

   _____

   -

   _____

3. can   hear   we   thunder

   _____

   -

   _____

4. on   its   way   is   storm   a

   _____

   -

   _____

5. have   to   we   will   get   inside

   _____

   -

   _____

6. read   can   we   books   some   good

   _____

   -

     FS123301 Grammar Made Simple Grade 2 ▪ © Frank Schaffer Publications, Inc.

Capital **I**

The word **I** is always capitalized. Use it when you talk about yourself, instead of saying your name. Example:

> **I** like to sing.

Write a complete sentence to answer each question. Use the word **I** in your answer.

1. Who are you?

   ----

2. How old are you?

   ----

3. What kind of pet would you like?

   ----

4. What do you like to eat?

   ----

5. What do you want to be someday?

Titles for People

- The titles **Mr., Mrs., Ms.,** and **Dr.** begin with a capital letter and end with a period.
- The title **Miss** begins with a capital letter but does not have a period.
- **Initials** are capital letters and end with a period.

Write the names correctly from the box onto
the business cards.

miss j lopez	**mrs jackson**	**mr l k wall**
dr rossi	**ms m goodman**	**miss chang**

Book Titles

The **first** word, the **last** word, and all **important** words in the title of a book or story have a capital letter. Examples:

Alex and the Birthday Dog
The New Friend

Write each book title correctly, using capital letters where they are needed.

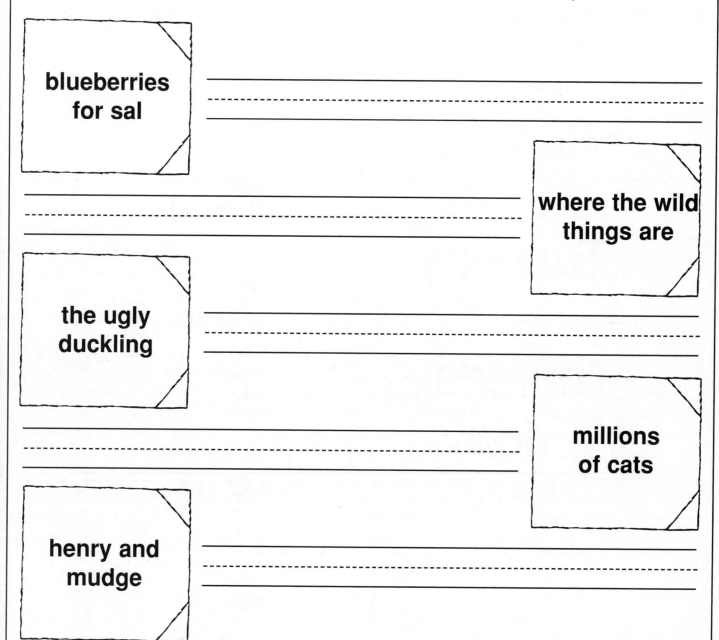

blueberries for sal

where the wild things are

the ugly duckling

millions of cats

henry and mudge

Days of the Week

Days of the week begin with a capital letter.
Sunday Monday Tuesday Wednesday Thursday Friday Saturday
Abbreviations for the days of the week begin with a capital letter and end with a period.

Sun. Mon. Tues. Wed. Thurs. Fri. Sat.

Complete the lists by writing the missing days of the week and their abbreviations.

Name	Abbreviation
Sunday	
	Mon.
Tuesday	
	Wed.
Thursday	
Friday	
	Sat.

 FS123301 Grammar Made Simple Grade 2 ▪ © Frank Schaffer Publications, Inc.

Months of the **Y**ear

The names of the **months** begin with a capital letter.

January **February** **March** **April** **May** **June**

July **August** **September** **October** **November** **December**

Write the name of the month to finish each sentence.

1. _____ is the first month of the year.

2. We fly our flag on the 4th of _____ .

3. Mother's Day is in _____ .

4. Halloween is the last day of _____ .

5. I will give you a valentine in _____ .

6. _____ is the month for eating turkey.

Holidays

The names of **holidays** begin with a capital letter.
Write the name of each holiday below the picture that goes with it.

new year's day	president's day
valentine's day	thanksgiving
halloween	fourth of july

_____   _____

-   -

_____   _____

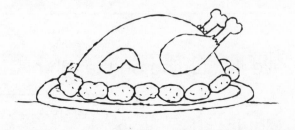

_____   _____

-   -

_____   _____

_____   _____

-   -

_____   _____

FS123301 Grammar Made Simple Grade 2 ▪ © Frank Schaffer Publications, Inc.

Name _____

Proper Names

Proper names are names of special people, places, and things.
Proper names begin with a capital letter.
Read the sentences carefully.
Draw three lines under each letter that should be a capital.
Example:

Dad and ann are going to pinewood park.

Will aunt clara's dog peaches go, too?

1. Mother is taking us to scott city today.

2. We will take bibby to the vet.

3. Then we will stop at dot's bakery.

4. Mother will order a cake for grandma rose's birthday.

5. Terry and I want to go to tiny tales bookstore.

6. We have to stop at ford's car wash.

Write the names of four places found above.

_____   _____

_____   _____

_____   _____

Seasons of the Year

You know that the names of days, months, and holidays have a capital letter at the beginning. Be careful! The names of the seasons do not have a capital letter. They begin with a small letter.

summer fall winter spring

Read each sentence carefully.
Draw a line through a letter that should be small.

This $ummer Jason will take swimming lessons.

Draw three lines under a letter that should be capital.

The month of <u>august</u> is sunny and hot.

1. On thursday we play soccer.

2. Benjamin likes Spring because he can play baseball.

3. Ice skating is my favorite Winter sport.

4. In may we are going to watch the car races.

5. We played ball at the father's day picnic.

6. Do you think Fall is a good time for basketball?

Write the names of the four seasons.

_____   _____

_____   _____

FS123301 Grammar Made Simple Grade 2 ▪ © Frank Schaffer Publications, Inc.

Usage

Familiarize your students with the rules of proper usage. Give them practice in properly using words such as *I* and *me*; *its* and *it's*; and *see, saw,* and *seen.*

MASTER YOUR MANNERS
Partner Activity

Teach your students that when using the word *I* along with the name of another person, it is good manners (and correct usage) to put the other person's name first. For example, *Travis and I are going to the fair.* Have the children pair up for this activity. Ask the children to talk with their partners and find something that they both like to do. Have them each write a sentence that uses *I* and their partner's name, following this pattern: *Maggie and I like to jump rope.* Then give each pair an opportunity to read their sentences to the class. The same activity can be used on another day to reinforce correct usage of the word *me.*

SAW OR SEEN?
Art Activity

A sentence-making activity will introduce your students to proper usage of the words *see, sees, saw,* and *seen.* Write several sentences using those words on sentence strips, then cut them apart. Make two "helper puppets" from craft sticks. To make the puppets, glue on a circle for a head and draw a face on it. Glue a triangle below the face on one puppet and a rectangle on the other, for bodies. Write *has* on one, and *have* on the other. Explain to the class that these words are the "helpers" that must help the word *seen* whenever it appears in a sentence. Distribute the word cards for the first sentence and have the children holding them stand in sentence order where the class can see them. Give the helper puppets to two volunteers, and ask the class to tell if a helper is needed. If so, the child holding the helper word stands in the sentence with the other children while the class reads it aloud. Repeat with different sentences and different children holding the word cards and puppets.

We see the new truck.

Jay (has) seen my old car.

Our friends (have) seen your picture.

Who saw the picture of the new truck?

I (have) seen his blue truck.

You (have) seen our old one.

Name Yourself Last

When using the words **I** or **me**, it is good manners to put yourself last.
Example: **Joe and I** take the bus to school.
Today Mother drove **Joe and me** to school.

Read each pair of sentences. Draw a line under the correct sentence.

1. I and Jody are going to Wonderland.

2. Jody and I are going to Wonderland.

3. Jason, Maria, and I are in the same class.

4. Jason, I, and Maria are in the same class.

5. Dad took Belle and me to the library.

6. Dad took me and Belle to the library.

7. Mom has treats for me, Alex, and Chucky.

8. Mom has treats for Alex, Chucky, and me.

Write your own sentence about yourself and a friend. Put yourself last.

_____

_____

    FS123301 Grammar Made Simple Grade 2 ■ © Frank Schaffer Publications, Inc.

Using I and Me

I and **me** are words that take the place of your name.
Use **I** to tell something you do, you are, or you feel.
Use **me** to tell something done to you, by you, for you, or with you.

Example: **I** am a good runner.
My friend runs with **me.**

Write **I** or **me** in each sentence.

1. Jill and _____ like to paint.

2. She gave _____ a new paint set.

3. Mother lets _____ paint after school.

4. Sometimes Jill paints with _____ .

5. Things get messy when _____ paint.

6. Mother and _____ clean up the mess.

Name _____

Saw and Seen

The word **seen** needs a helper in front of it. Two of its helpers are **have** and **has**. Example:

      You **have seen** the little calf.
      Tommy **has seen** the mother cow.

The word **saw** does not need a helper.
Example:

      We **saw** cows on the farm.

Write **saw, seen, has,** or **have** in each sentence to finish it correctly.

1. On her way to school, Lisa _____ Mrs. Fine's cat.

2. Every day this week, Lisa _____ **seen** the cat.

3. I _____ **seen** it, too.

4. We **have** _____ that cat in the window.

5. What is the name of that cat Lisa **has** _____ ?

6. When it _____ us, the cat swished its tail.

      FS123301 Grammar Made Simple Grade 2 ▪ © Frank Schaffer Publications, Inc.

Its and It's

The words **it's** and **its** sound the same but are spelled differently.
They have different meanings:

It's means **it is**
Its means **belongs to it**

Read the story. Circle in **red** the words that mean **it is.** Circle in **blue** the words that mean **belongs to it.**

A Robin Family

Winter is over. It's spring.

A robin is building its nest.

The robin sings while it's working.

Its song tells other robins to keep away.

The robin guards its home.

But one robin keeps coming back. It's the robin's mate.

Soon there will be a robin family living in its own nest.

Write your own sentence about the robin. Use **it's** or **its.**

_____

_____

_____

Usage

Continue your study of the rules of proper usage by emphasizing proper use of the words *good* and *well,* and *can* and *may*. Use these activities to give students written and oral language practice.

WHAT DID YOU SAY?

Game

Play a simple movement game to reinforce the distinction between the words *can* and *may* and to emphasize careful listening. Explain to the children that *can* means *able to*, and *may* is used to show possibility or to ask permission. Introduce the game by having the children stand in a large, open space. One student asks a question such as "May we nod our heads?" Your reply can be, "Yes, you can nod your heads." In this case, no one should move. If you say, "Yes, you may nod your heads," everyone may move. Anyone you catch moving when not allowed is out.

IT'S ALL WELL AND GOOD

Class Activity

Give your students practice in using the words *well* and *good* with this writing activity. Discuss the uses of the two words—*well* describes how an action is done (a verb); *good* describes a person, place, or thing (a noun). Write the following sentence frames on the board.

> Tran can <u>write well</u>.
>
> Tran is a <u>good writer</u>.

Then ask someone to underline the action word plus *well* in the first sentence. Have another student underline the person, place, or thing plus *good* in the second sentence. Give the children several other examples. Then ask them to think of things they can do well. Have them use the sentence frames to write about themselves at the bottom of a sheet of drawing paper. Ask them to illustrate their sentences. Then assemble the children's papers between tagboard covers to make a class book. Title it "Well and Good." Place the book in your classroom reading corner for children to enjoy during independent reading time.

Good and Well

Use the word **good** to describe a person, place, or thing.
Example:

> My brother is a **good** dancer.

Use the word **well** to describe how an action is done.
Example:

> Alan dances **well.**

Color a popcorn kernel to show which word belongs in each sentence.

1. My friend Rosa cooks everything _____ .

2. Rosa makes _____ popcorn.

3. She uses a _____ pan.   good   well

4. She heats the oil _____ .   good

5. She gives the pan a _____ shake.   good

6. The popcorn tastes _____ .   good

7. We clean the bowl _____ .   good

8. Rosa is my _____ friend.   good

Name _____

Can or May

The word **can** means **able to.** Example:
    Jeff **can** skate fast.

The word **may** is used for **permission.** Example:
    You **may** use my skates.

Write **can** or **may** in each blank to finish the cartoon.

_____ you open this jar for me?

Mom, _____ I go ouside with Ryan?

Dad said we _____ each have one.

I _____ borrow and carry.

Class, you _____ line up now.

We _____ not play outside today.

FS123301 Grammar Made Simple Grade 2 ■ © Frank Schaffer Publications, Inc.

Usage

Help your students learn when to use common homophones such as *to, too,* **and** *two; their, there,* **and** *they're.*

HOMOPHONES

Homophones are words that sound alike but are spelled differently. Many riddles and jokes are based on homophones. Here are some examples:

When is a boat like a store? Answer: When it has sales.

Where can you find a load of bubble gum? Answer: On a chew-chew train.

Have your students read books of jokes and riddles to find homophones. Once a day, add the homophones to a class list you keep on chart paper. Children will enjoy the special time to share jokes and riddles, and it will reinforce their skills in proper word usage.

Literature suggestion: Read to your students the humorous book *The King Who Rained* by Fred Gwyne (Prentice-Hall, 1988) as part of your study of homophones.

SAME SOUND, DIFFERENT SPELLING

Children enjoy making books of homophones. Have them fold several sheets of paper in half and staple the folded edge to make a book. Brainstorm a list of homophones with the class. (See suggestions below.) Show the children how to write each pair of homophones, with one word to a page, on facing pages. They can draw a picture for each word.

cent (penny)	sent (did send)
buy (purchase)	bye (farewell)
chilly (cool)	chili (food)
fir (tree)	fur (on an animal)
hair (on head)	hare (rabbit)
lay (recline)	lei (flower necklace)
road (street)	rode (from ride)
shoe (covers foot)	shoo (chase away)

To, Too, and Two

The words **to, too,** and **two** are homophones. They sound the same but are spelled differently. Here is how to remember which one to use:

to	**too**	**two**
toward, direction	also	the number 2

Read the pen pal letters. Write **to, too,** or **two** in each blank.

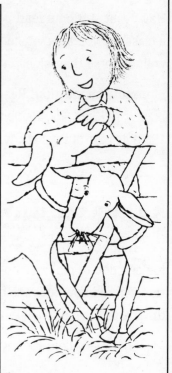

Dear Pen Pal,

My name is Holly. I live on a farm. I have

_____ goats. I have a cat, _____. I like

milking the goats. I like putting the milk on my

cereal. My cat Inky likes the milk, _____ . In _____

weeks we will take my goats _____ the fair.

Please write soon.

Your friend,
Holly

Dear Holly,

My name is Amber. I have a cat, _____ . My cat has _____

black feet and _____ white feet. I hope I can meet your goats.

I would drink some milk, _____.

Your friend,
Amber

FS123301 Grammar Made Simple Grade 2 ▪ © Frank Schaffer Publications, Inc.

Name _____

There, Their, They're

The words **there**, **their**, and **they're** are homophones. They sound the same but are spelled differently. Here is how to remember them:

there a place	**their** belonging to them	**they're** they are

Finish the story by writing **there, their,** or **they're** in each blank.

Lori and Tom work in a supermarket bakery.

_____ job is to bake rolls.

_____ putting frozen rolls onto trays.

The trays go into a cooler. The rolls will thaw _____ .

Late at night _____ taken out.

Now the rolls go into the steamer. The rolls get puffy. Tom takes them out of

_____ and puts them in the oven.

After _____ baked, Lori puts the rolls in bags.

People come to the bakery to get rolls for _____ dinners.

Proofreading Skills

Give students practice in eliminating extra words from their speech and writing. Learning some basic proofreading marks will help your students become more aware of carefully checking their work.

TOO MANY WORDS Group Activity

Language learning is a gradual, developmental process. Guide your students along the path to more precise speaking and writing by making them aware of the extra words that are sometimes used in children's everyday language. Focus on the words *to, at, of, he/she,* and *more* in this exercise. Have the children work in groups. Give each group a sentence written on a sentence strip. Have the groups cut apart the sentences into words. Then have the students in each group work together to decide which word in the sentence could be dropped without changing the meaning of the sentence. Have the group stand before the class with each group member holding a word card. The class may read the sentence aloud. Then have the child holding the unnecessary word drop out. Read the sentence together again and discuss it. Do the same for each group's sentence.

Sample sentences:

Where is Maria at? (at)

The cat jumped off of the wall. (of)

Where is Andy going to? (to)

My sister she plays soccer. (she)

My dog is more bigger than yours. (more)

PROOFREADER'S MARKS Class Activity

Give your students high marks for proofreading their own work. Draw their attention to the importance of checking their work by teaching them some basic proofreader's marks. (See chart on page 74.) Explain that these marks are used by editors when they check materials to be published. Post a large chart with proofreader's marks where children can reference it. Encourage the children to use the marks before turning in their papers, or anytime you have them exchange papers to check each other's work.

∧   Put in letters or words.

/   Change to a small letter.

≡   Change to a capital letter.

ℊ   Take out a word or words.

Too Many Words

Sometimes sentences have extra words in them. The extra words can be taken out without changing the meaning of the sentence. Look for words like **to, at, of, he, she, got,** and **more**. They may be extra words.

Examples: Where are you going **to**?
              Where is Mother **at**?

We can take out the extra words with a mark like this:
              I have **got** a new bike.
              It is **more** better than my old one.

Use this mark 𝒈 to take out the extra word in each sentence.
Write the sentence without the extra word.

1. My dad he has a racing bike.

_____

_____

2. The glass fell off of the table.

_____

_____

3. This truck is more bigger than his.

_____

_____

4. Where is Alaska at?

_____

_____

5. I don't know where he went to.

_____

_____

Proofreading Marks

Always read over your work. When you read over something you have written, it is called **proofreading.** Use these marks when you are proofreading.

Mark	What It Means
ℰ	Take out a word or words.
/	Change to a small letter.
≡	Change to a capital letter.
∧	Put in letters or words.

Examples:

Take out the word **she.**

My sister she likes carrots.

Change **W** to a small letter.

I think Winter is here.

Change **j** to a capital letter.

Father's Day is in june.

Put in the word **very.**

very
It is a cold day.

FS123301 Grammar Made Simple Grade 2 ▪ © Frank Schaffer Publications, Inc.

Check Your Work

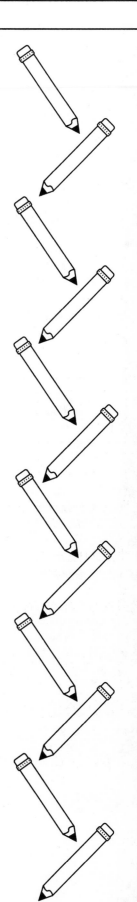

☐   1. My name is on my paper.

☐   2. My writing is neat.

☐   3. I followed directions.

☐   4. I checked my answers.

☐   5. Sentences begin with a capital letter.

☐   6. Sentences end with punctuation marks.

☐   7. Sentences are complete thoughts.

☐   8. My spelling is correct.

☐   9. My grammar is correct.

☐   10. This is my best work.

Answer Key

Page 4
Answers will vary. Students will make noun books and fill them with nouns they find.

Page 5
Proper nouns (top of page): Uncle John, Miss Sanchez, Lakeview Mall, Matt Hart, Green Grove Library, Ohio, City Science Center
Proper nouns (bottom of page): Saturday, Aunt Marie, Brookside Museum, Willow Park, Riviera Station

Page 6
One: boy, slide, bike, dog, net
More than one: girls, bars, bushes, swings, balls

Page 7
treat/treats
friend/friends
box/boxes
branch/branches
class/classes
1. boxes
2. classes
3. treats
4. branches
5. friends

Page 10
Dogs bark.
Snow falls.
Sun shines.
Birds chirp.
Girls skate.
Plants grow.

Page 11
Across
1. spray
2. rolls
3. soaks
4. drops
5. crash
Down
1. splash
6. run
7. drips
8. flow
9. shoots

Page 12
stuffed
sewed
brushed
dressed
packed
mailed

Page 13
1. am
2. are
3. are
4. is
5. is
6. are

Page 14
1. wore
2. fell
3. slept
4. went
5. built
6. threw

Page 17
Game instructions are on page 16.

Page 18
we
They
It
us
He
mine

Page 19

Pronoun	Picture
He	Grandpa
It	hoe
They	plants
You	Niki
it	watering can
Our	Grandpa and Niki

Page 22
1. sticky
2. silk
3. strong
4. giant
5. juicy
6. delicious
big, blue
eight, hairy
Students will complete the pictures.

Page 23
1. brown
2. glass
3. noisy
4. delicious
5. hot
6. good
7. sweet
8. ticking
9. warm
10. tasty
looks: brown, glass
sounds: noisy, ticking
smells: good, sweet
tastes: delicious, tasty
feels: hot, warm

Page 24
1. bigger
2. younger
3. faster
4. slower
5. tallest
6. fastest
7. smallest

Page 25
1. Our class went to the Nature Center.
2. We saw nests and other animal homes.
3. We followed a long path.
4. There were many flowers blooming.
5. We found a quiet place to sketch.
6. I drew a spotted butterfly on a flower.

Page 26
warm
red
hard
pink
loud
furry
round
1. older
2. oldest
3. brighter
4. brightest

Page 28
1. an
2. a
3. a
4. an
5. an
6. a
7. a
8. an
9. an
10. an
11. a
12. a
13. a
14. a

Page 29
1. an
2. an
3. a
4. an
5. A
6. a

Page 31
Answers will vary. Students may choose any adverb from the box to complete the sentences.

Page 32
1. yesterday
2. outside
3. nicely
4. today
5. inside
6. carefully
7. gently
8. nearby
9. tomorrow
Where: outside, inside, nearby
How: nicely, carefully, gently
When: yesterday, today, tomorrow

Page 34
1 Claire . . .
3 Here . . .
1 This. . .
3 I like . . .
2 We . . .
2 Some animals . . .
1 Some animals are . . .
3 Ray . . .
2 He . . .
2 What . . .

Page 35
3 A winter . . .
1 I look . . .
2 Walk . . .
3 Look . . .
1 They . . .
2 The rabbit . . .
2 It hopped . . .
1 You can . . .
2 Wait . . .
3 Did . . .

Page 38
Our class is on the playground.
I saw a blue butterfly.
We are going camping.
Dinosaurs lived long ago.
Dan is reading a new book.

Page 39
1. Dad and I
2. The kite
3. A good wind
4. The sun
5. Pepper Park
6. Our picnic lunch

Page 40
1. rakes
2. pile
3. looks
4. scrapes
5. want
6. rides
7. help
8. begins

Page 41
1. recycles newspapers
2. fills up fast
3. are collected on Friday
4. help collect them
5. gives one class a prize

Page 44
1. We see a rainbow.
2. There must be rain and sun.
3. Sunlight has many colors.
4. Raindrops split the sunlight.
5. We see the colors.
6. They make a rainbow.

Page 45
Questions will vary. Each question should begin with a capital and end with a question mark.

Page 46
1. Let's go!
2. Look who's here!
3. Watch me!
4. What a mess!
5. Wake up!
6. Watch out!

Page 47
1. Wash your hands.
2. Hang it here.
3. Ring the bell.
4. Close the window.
5. Open your books.
6. Have one.

Page 48
1. Can Belle read her book?
2. Belle can read her book.
1. Does this train go to the depot?
2. This train does go to the depot.
1. Are Mark and Lisa playing baseball?
2. Mark and Lisa are playing baseball.

Page 49
Quotation marks should be inserted in the story as shown here.

"Who is crossing my bridge?" asked the Troll.
"It is little Billy Goat Gruff," answered the goat.
"I will eat you up," said the Troll.
The little goat said, "Wait for the second Billy Goat Gruff. He's much bigger than I."
So the Troll waited for the next Billy Goat Gruff.
"Now who is crossing my bridge?" asked the Troll.
"I am the second Billy Goat Gruff," answered the goat.
"I will eat you up," said the Troll.
The second goat said, "Wait for the third Billy Goat Gruff. He's much bigger."
Thinking he would get a bigger meal, the Troll waited.
"Who is tramping across my bridge?" asked the Troll.
"I am the third Billy Goat Gruff," answered the next goat.
The Troll growled, "I am coming to eat you up!"
"Oh no, you're not," said the biggest Billy Goat Gruff. And he tossed the Troll off the bridge with his big horns.

Page 52
1. The sun was out this morning.
2. Now we see gray clouds.
3. We can hear thunder.
4. A storm is on its way.
5. We will have to get inside.
6. We can read some good books.

Page 53
Answers will vary. Each answer should contain the word *I*.

Page 54
Miss J. Lopez
Dr. Rossi
Mrs. Jackson
Ms. M. Goodman
Mr. L. K. Wall
Miss Chang

Page 55
Blueberries for Sal
Where the Wild Things Are
The Ugly Duckling
Millions of Cats
Henry and Mudge

Page 56
Sun.
Monday
Tues.
Wednesday
Thurs.
Fri.
Saturday

Page 57
1. January
2. July
3. May
4. October
5. February
6. November

Page 58
1. Halloween
2. Valentine's Day
3. President's Day
4. Fourth of July
5. Thanksgiving
6. New Year's Day

Page 59
1. Scott City
2. Bibby
3. Dot's Bakery
4. Grandma Rose's
5. Tiny Tales Bookstore
6. Ford's Car Wash
Four places: Scott City, Dot's Bakery, Tiny Tales Bookstore, Ford's Car Wash

Page 60
1. Thursday
2. spring
3. winter
4. May
5. Father's Day Picnic
6. fall
summer, fall, winter, spring

Page 62
2. Jody and I are going to Wonderland.
3. Jason, Maria, and I are in the same class.
5. Dad took Belle and me to the library.
8. Mom has treats for Alex, Chucky, and me.
Sentences will vary.

Page 63
1. I
2. me
3. me
4. me
5. I
6. I

Page 64
1. saw
2. has
3. have
4. seen
5. seen
6. saw

Page 65
It's spring. (red)
A robin is building its nest. (blue)
The robin sings while it's working. (red)
Its song tells other robins to keep away. (blue)
The robin guards its home. (blue)
It's the robin's mate. (red)
Soon there will be a robin family living in its own nest. (blue)
Sentences will vary.

Page 67
1. well
2. good
3. good
4. well
5. good
6. good
7. well
8. good

Page 68
Can you open this jar for me?
Dad said we may each have one.
Class, you may line up now.
Mom, may I go outside with Ryan?
I can borrow and carry.
We can not play outside today.

Page 70
I have two goats.
I have a cat, too.
My cat Inky likes the milk, too.
In two weeks we will take my goats to the fair.

I have a cat, too.
My cat has two black feet and two white feet.
I would drink some milk, too.

Page 71
Their job is . . .
They're putting frozen . . .
The rolls will thaw there.
Late at night they're . . .
Tom takes them out of there . . .
After they're baked . . .
People . . . for their dinners.

Page 73
1. he: My dad has a racing bike
2. of: The glass fell off the table.
3. more: This truck is bigger than his.
4. at: Where is Alaska?
5. to: I don't know where he went.